AWS

CERTIFIED SOLUTIONS ARCHITECT ASSOCIATE (SAA-C02)

AWS Certified Solutions Architect Associate Ultimate Cheat Sheet, Practice Test Questions with Detailed Explanations and Links

HILLARY MORRISON

TABLE OF CONTENTS

Introduction

The AWS Certified Solutions Architect Associate (SAA-C02) certification is one of the most sought after for IT professionals. For those employees that get the SAA-CO2 qualifications, it opens the door for greater advancement within their careers. Career advancement comes with many benefits, including a significant increase in salary as Certified Solution Architects command higher salaries.

Anyone can take the course and attempt the exam. However, it is more suited to IT professionals who already have an in-depth knowledge of cloud infrastructure, deployment, and design. The student needs to have at least one year of hands-on experience in wide-area networking or, more preferably, cloud-based system solutions. This is only a recommendation though, as stated previously, anyone can take the course and exam. If you are new to the infrastructure and AWS before trying this course, you should look into doing the AWS Certified Cloud Practitioner exam first. This will give you a better basis to work on and a greater understanding of AWS.

AWS Certified Solutions Architect Associate (SAA-CO2)

The AWS Certified Solutions Architect Associate (SAA-CO2) is not an easy exam to pass, and the student needs to put a good few months of hard preparation and study into passing it. The tester must go over their work several times, making sure they fully understand the content.

It will also help a great deal if the student can work in a lab environment to get hands-on experience with the study material. Although the student may already work in an AWS environment, it is best to keep learning in a controlled lab type environment. For the sake of the course and exam, they require students to assess and answer questions based on various scenarios. It is safe to say, while they may build these situations around real-word ones, they will not mimic any live environments the student may work in.

Different Ways to Take the Course

To do the course you can sign up with Amazon at the following website link:

> https://aws.amazon.com/certification/certified-solutions-architect-associate/

For more information on how the course will run, you can get this information from the following website link:

> https://aws.amazon.com/certification/certification-prep/

Creating an AWS account is quick, simple, and free of charge. There are, however, some fees involved for specific courses, exams, or exam simulators offered by AWS.

Benefits of Becoming an AWS Certified Solutions Architect Associate (SAA-C02)

There are numerous benefits for becoming an AWS Certified Solutions Architect Associate for both the IT professional or aspiring IT professional.

These benefits include:

- Better career opportunities

- Career advancement opportunities

- Higher pay structure

- Demonstrates the holder of the certificate's expertise in the field

- Gives the IT professional more credibility

- Makes an IT resume stand out from the rest

What to Expect

The course covers all the basic material that the learner will find in the materials they receive. The best route is a classroom-based course that covers:

- AWS Technical Essentials

- Architecting on AWS

- Architecting on AWS - Accelerator

AWS also offers the Exam Readiness training, which can be done as either:

- Classroom training—This is given either a virtual or physical classroom training environment with an accredited and certified AWS instructor.

- Digital training—This can be taken through AWS, and the learner can take the course as it suits them.

- Webinars—An AWS-accredited instructor leads scheduled webinars with question and answer sessions after the webinar is done.

This book will help you:

- Identify key topics that are required for the exam from each of the four domains.

- Read questions and identify keywords before choosing an answer during the exam.

- Practice the exam with actual exam-type questions.

The Goal of the AWS Certified Solutions Architect

The course is designed to teach cloud solutions architects how to create architectures that fill the requirements of the 4 AWS Domains covered in this course.

By the end of the course and exam, the cloud solutions architect must be able to create AWS architectures that are:

- Resilient

- Performant

- Secure

- Cost-optimized

- Offer operation excellence

Chapter 1

Exams

There are 65 questions when taking the SAA-CO2 exam for which you have 130 minutes to complete. The exam is scored from 100 to 1000 points, and the student needs to have scored 720 or higher to pass.

If the exam is not passed, it can be taken again five days after the previous exam. Upon successful completion of the exam, the certification is valid for two years, after which recertification is required at a reduced cost to the student.

The following are where the exam can be taken and each facility has test simulators for the SAA-CO2:

- AWS — https://www.aws.training/certification

- Pearsons VUE - https://home.pearsonvue.com/aws/onvue

AWS SAA-CO2 Exam Question Allocation Table Content Outline

The exam has the following content domains that each make up a percentage of the exam:

Domain 1: Design Resilient Architectures, which makes up 30% of the exams.

This domain consists of the following topics or concepts for resilient AWS architectures:

- The learner must be able to design a multi-tier architecture solution.

- The learner must be able to design highly available and fault-tolerant architectures.

- Using AWS service, the learner must be able to design decoupling mechanisms.

- The learning is required to know how to choose appropriate resilient storage.

Domain 2: Design High-Performing Architectures which makes up 28% of the exams.

This domain consists of the following topics or concepts pertaining to a workload:

- Identify scalable and elastic compute solutions for a workload.

- Select scalable and high-performing storage solutions for a workload.

- Select networking solutions based on high-performance for a workload.

- Select database solutions for a workload that are high-performance.

Domain 3: Design Secure Applications and Architectures, which makes up 24% of the exams.

This domain consists of the following topics or concepts about security:

- The learner must be able to design secure access to AWS resources.

- The learners must understand and be able to design secure application tiers.

- The learner must be confident enough to select appropriate data security options.

Domain 4: Design Cost-Optimized Architectures which makes up 18% of the exams.

This domain consists of the following topics or concepts about cost-optimization of AWS:

- This domain requires the student to be able to identify cost-effective storage solutions.

- The student must know how to identify database services and compute cost-effective services.

- The student must be able to expertly design cost-effective network architectures.

What to Expect From the Exam

To do well and pass the exam, the student is expected to know the AWS core services and how to use them to create systems that follow AWS best practices.

Every missed answer is marked as an incorrect answer, and an incorrect answer will bring down the overall score of the exam.

A question can be marked for future consideration, but try and guess what you think it may be before moving on to the next question. That way, if time runs out and you have not had a chance to go back to review the question, you have a chance of getting it right as opposed to not answering it at all.

At the end of the exam, you can review each answer and questions you have marked for review. Marking a question for review also makes it easier to get back to, especially when time is running short.

It is important to keep an eye on the time periodically throughout the exam, and if you feel you are spending too much time on a question, mark it for review rather than keep going back to it.

The exam content will contain questions that are broken down into **Response Types** and **Unscored Content**.

When taking the exams, it is vital to remember that all the details on the test questions may count.

Response Types

The examination is broken down into two types of questions that will be asked of the student. These questions are:

- **Multiple choice questions**—These questions only have one correct answer but the student will be given a choice of four answers to choose from. The three incorrect answers are what are known as **distractor** answers.

Example:

Q1: What is the color of the sky?

      A. Orange

      B. Green

C. Azure

D. Lemon

Answer: C. Azure

- **Multiple response questions**—These types usually have one question with 5 to 6 answers to choose from. It will be stated how many correct answers to choose from the list of given answers. For instance, the question may say something like, from the following list, choose the two correct answers.

Example:

Q2: What are the parts of a motor car?

Choose two.

    A. Seat

    B. Jar

    C. Engine

    D. Lid

    E. Bag

    Answer: A. Seat & C. Engine

Not all of the questions will be ones that have obvious answers that stand out. Some of the questions will require the exam taker to choose the right procedure or solution for the scenario put forward in the matter.

Example:

Q3: Mary needs to make some toast with butter and jam. From the options below, choose the procedure that best explains how to make the buttered toast.

>
> A. Put the bread on the plate and butter it with fresh butter.
>
> B. Put the butter and bread on the plate with a knife.
>
> C. Put the bread and butter in the oven on high for 20 minutes.
>
> D. Put the bread in the toaster, and when it pops out, put it on a plate and butter the bread.

Answer: D. Put the bread in the toaster and when it pops out, put it on a plate and butter the bread.

Work through the questions by eliminating answers that you are sure do not pertain to the question. If you know the subject well enough, the incorrect answers will be more clear. There are always two answers that will look pretty similar. They need to be read through really carefully because this is what trips a student up.

Unscored Content

There may be what is called unscored content included on the exam. Although they do not affect the exam takers score they are there to gather statistical information.

End of the Exam

It is a good idea to flag questions you had doubts about, so if you have time at the end of the exam you can review them.

At the end of the exam, the student will receive their mark and whether or not they passed the exam. They will also get the statistics on what their strengths and weaknesses were for the subject based on answers.

Whether the student passes or fails the exam, the strength and weakness table is a valuable tool. It will show the learner what they need to work on within the AWS domain to continue focusing on.

Do not let it discourage you if you did not pass the first time around, not many people do. But you will know what you need to go back and work on to ensure you do pass the next time around.

How to Choose the Best Answer for Exam Questions

This section will cover some question strategies that will help the student identify and consider when choosing an answer to exam questions.

If you find you do not understand or recognize a concept, system, or core service during practice tests, go back and study it. A term, idea, or service you are not familiar with is a sure sign that you are not ready to take the full exam. This is one of the reasons exam simulators and practice tests are so important to any student.

It is also good to realize that practice tests and test simulations are not going to be exactly the same as the exam. But the way in which you need to strategize the answers and the thought process that goes into each question will be the same.

Good Exam Answering Strategy:

- Before answering, read both the questions and answers through and make sure you understand it.

- Look for key features that may match both the question and the answer.

- Rule out any answer that you know for certain does not pertain to or could be the correct answer. Leave only those answers that may have some bearing on the question.

- Always pay attention to qualifying clauses as these are put there to see if the test taker is paying attention to detail. For instance, the question may be for the **most cost-effective, efficient solution**, which is not always the most suitable. If a company is tightening up on costs, they may not always be looking for the best solution but the one that offers them the most value.

- If the answer pertains to AWS core services, look for clues in the question.

Chapter 2

Design Resilient Architectures

Domain 1 of the SAA-CO2 exam requires the student to effectively design reliable and resilient AWS architectures.

This chapter will discuss how to design resilient architecture, best practices, and the key points that the student should not miss for the exam. At the end of the chapter, there are a few helpful test questions to test your knowledge on the topics and concepts discussed throughout the chapter.

Best Practices for Designing Resilient Architectures

To create a reliable and resilient AWS Architecture Solution, the following practices should be taken into account:

- Storage should be chosen for its resilience and reliability.

- The design should offer high fault tolerance and availability.

- Multi-tier solutions should be designed to fit the needs of the system.

- Determine how to use AWS services when designing decoupling mechanisms.

Storage

A resilient system means that in the event of downtime or a disaster, the system does not lose any data or state. When choosing storage solutions, it should be done with this in mind.

EC2 Instance Store

- Instance store is found on the physical hard drive where the EC2 compute services for AWS run.

- The Instance Store has ephemeral volumes, which means that when the instance running them stops, any instance stored on the volume is lost.

- Not all EC2 instances offer Instance Stores.

- Because the Instance Store is on the physical drive the disk size/capacity is fixed.

- The disk size/capacity of the Instance Store depends on the type of EC2 instance.

- The disk type also depends on the type of EC2 instance.

- Instance stores are only reliable while the application is running, so it only offers application-level durability.

- Instance store should only be used for storing temporary data while the application is running, or is to be replicated elsewhere. Because it is ephemeral, it is fast and effective for replications.

- Instance sore is also good to use for caching.

Elastic Block Store (EBS)

- EBS only connects to one EC2 instance at a time.

- EBS is attachable storage that supports both encryption and snapshots.

- There are different types of EBS solutions.

- EBS is not dependent on the EC2 instance as it has an independent lifecycle. This means that even when you stop the EC2 instance the EBS volume gets preserved.

- You can configure some types of EBS volumes for larger or smaller read writes per second as it supports provisioning IOPS.

- EBS can be attached to multiple volumes which can create larger volumes by using IOPS with Raid 0 and striping.

- EBS is attachable storage for an EC2 instance that is both reliable and durable.

- EBS Solid-State Drive (SSD) Volume Types (good for random access):

  o General Purpose SSD (gp2)

    - Use cases include Development and testing environments, virtual desktops, low-latency interactive applications, and system boot volumes. This volume type works well for nearly all workloads.

    - Volume size is 1GB to 16TB

    - Maximum IOPS per volume is 10,000

    - Maximum throughput per volume is 160 MB per second

    - Performance attribute = IOPS

  o Provisioned IOPS SSD (io1)

    - Use cases include Large database workloads, business-critical applications that need sustained IOPS, high-performance throughput per volume of up to 160 MB per second, or 10,000 IOPS.

    - Volume size is 4GB to 16TB

- Maximum IOPS per volume is 32,000

- Maximum throughput per volume is 500 MB per second

- Performance attribute = IOPS

- EBS Hard disk Drives (HDD) Volume Types (good for sequential access):

  - Throughput Optimized HDD (st1)

    - Use cases include: This volume cannot be used as a boot volume; it is best for data warehouses, big data, log processing, and streaming workloads.

    - Volume size is 500GB to 16TB

    - Maximum IOPS per volume is 500

    - Maximum throughput per volume is 500 MB per second

    - Performance attribute = MB per second

  - Cold HDD (sc1)

    - Use cases include: This volume cannot be used as a boot volume, best for storing large amounts of data **not** accessed frequently, and used as a low-cost storage solution.

- Volume size is 500GB to 16TB

- Maximum IOPS per volume is 250

- Maximum throughput per volume is 250 MB per second

- Performance attribute = MB per second

Elastic File System (EFS)

- EFS is the Amazon cloud storage solution.

- EFS is a shared storage solution.

- EFS allows for multiple EC2 instances to access the same EFS volume.

- EFS volumes are referred to as elastic volumes as the capacity can grow or shrink as required.

- EFS volumes are capable of Petabyte (PB) scale file system storage solutions.

- EFS volumes are:

- Compatible with Linux based-based AMIs for Amazon EC2

- Supports NFS v4.0 protocol

- Supports NFS v4.1 (NFSv4) protocol

- EFS does not support Windows

- Only a single VPC can attach to an EFS volume at a time.

- EFS is best for workloads that require large quantities of data. This is using analytical data as it can seamlessly process and analyze data on a large scale.

Amazon Simple Storage Services (S3)

- Amazon S3 is a solution that is available in any region, making it more desirable than solutions such as EBS that is only available in particular areas (Region Availability).

- Amazon S3 can store most file types, including images, videos, data, and analytics.

- It is an excellent option for hosting websites.

- Amazon S3 offers simple object-oriented storage whereby all data types are stored in native format.

- Amazon S3 is implemented as a scalable distributed system

- The Amazon S3 Consistency model is:

  - Strongly consistent for new objects—This means that when an object is first stored, it appears right away.

  - Eventually consistent for updates—When an existing object is updated, it may not be instantly pulled through. This can lead to system version problems.

- Amazon S3 has a few storage classes

  - Amazon S3 Standard

    - Cheaper for uploads and downloads (access).

  - Amazon S3 Standard-Infrequent Access (IA)

    - Cheaper for storage but more expensive for uploads and downloads.

- Amazon S3 server-side encryption (data at rest)

  - SSE-S3—S3 master key encrypts files on the server-side.

- SSE-KMS—KMS master key encrypts files on the server-side.

- SSE-C—Customer provided and managed key encrypts files on the server-side.

- Amazon S3 server-side encryptions (data in transit)

  - HTTPS

- Amazon S3 allows files to be versioned, meaning files that are updated or deleted may still be accessed.

- Amazon S3 is designed for 99.999999999% durability, which is high.

- Amazon S3 can be accessed from anywhere as it has an internet API.

- Amazon S3 has unlimited capacity; it has access control, and can perform multi-part uploads.

Amazon Glacier

- Amazon Glacier is a storage solution for data not accessed frequently, for instance, backups, historical data, archives, and vaults (collections of archives).

- Amazon Glacier has three types of retrieval types:

- Standard—A middle option where the cost and retrieval time depends on the amount of data stored.

- Expedited—Much faster but a more expensive option and can take up to 5 minutes.

- Bulk—The cheapest and most cumbersome option as it can take as long as 12 hours.

- With each retrieval type, one needs to decide between latency or cost. The less lag, the higher the cost.

- Amazon Glacier can set up life cycle policies that can move data from S3 to Glacier buckets after a certain time frame. This makes it easier to automatically archive historical data.

- Amazon Glacier has been designed for high durability, which is set at 99.999999999.

- Amazon Glacier is also available across all regions (Regional Availability).

NOTE:

It is important to know the differences between the Instance Store and EBS. For EBS, you will need to know which is the cheaper of the volume storage types and why there is a pricing difference.

You can find more information on this topic at the following website links.

> https://docs.aws.amazon.com/whitepapers/latest/aws-storage-services-overview/welcome.html

> https://docs.aws.amazon.com/whitepapers/latest/aws-storage-services-overview/amazon-ec2-instance-storage.html

> https://docs.aws.amazon.com/whitepapers/latest/aws-storage-services-overview/amazon-ebs.html

> https://docs.aws.amazon.com/whitepapers/latest/aws-storage-services-overview/amazon-efs.html

> https://docs.aws.amazon.com/whitepapers/latest/aws-storage-services-overview/amazon-s3.html

> https://docs.aws.amazon.com/whitepapers/latest/aws-storage-services-overview/amazon-glacier.html

> https://docs.aws.amazon.com/whitepapers/latest/aws-storage-services-overview/amazon-cloudfront.html

Fault Tolerance

Fault tolerance should be built into the system as a normal operational event instead of treating it as an exception or unusual event. This makes applications and systems continue to operate even during any unusual events or faults to keep providing its service and value to the organization or user.

Using AWS Services to create loosely coupled systems, you ensure that the system has high fault tolerance. By following the design concepts and the five pillars of AWS Well-Architected Framework, you can achieve a fault-tolerant resilient system.

NOTE:

You can find more information on this topic at the following website links.

https://aws.amazon.com/architecture/well-architected/

https://aws.amazon.com/blogs/apn/the-5-pillars-of-the-aws-well-architected-framework/

Multi-tier Solutions

Whenever possible, it is best to design systems with multi-tier solutions. This allows for more resilience in the system and offers a higher rate of availability. If the system is designed with the proper decoupling mechanisms, it ensures that any downtime or failure that may occur in one area will not affect another area.

CloudFormation is an AWS service that allows for the creation of a large deployment that can consist of several S3 buckets, RDS databases, EC2 instances, DynamoDB tables, and networks. CloudFormation uses JASON templates to describe the infrastructure that is required and then converts the templates into infrastructure. This is called a stack, a collection of AWS resources, making it very easy to produce multiple copies of your infrastructure.

A stack also makes it easy to update all of your resources as one single unit.

Using **Lambda** allows for fully managed compute services that can run stateless code for a timed event or in response to one.

NOTE:

You can find more information on this topic at the following website links.

https://docs.aws.amazon.com/cloudformation/

https://docs.aws.amazon.com/lambda/index.html

Decoupling Mechanisms

When designing the system, it is always best to use AWS services for decoupling mechanisms. In a multi-tier system, decoupling mechanisms ensure that if one tier fails, it does affect any of the other tiers because they become decoupled. This enables parts of the system not affected by a tier failure to carry on working.

A tightly coupled system has one or more dependencies on each other. This means if one of the services goes offline, the entire system goes offline. For instance, if you had a web server that the email service was reliant upon, if the web server or email was taken down or failed, neither systems would work.

If one of the AWS services was used to create a decoupling mechanism between the web server and the email service, it would continue to collect email and send it like normal. The email would queue in the SQS until the system was restored. No email would be lost.

AWS Simple Queue Services (SQS) can also be used when there are services that need queuing facilities like a logging service where decoupling needs to be used for scalability. If a database needs to process a high workload of logging requests, it can become overloaded and backed up. It could even drop data or crash the system. Using the decoupling mechanism, the queues can be queued in the SQS and then directed to different logging services that feed the database.

The more data there is, the more logging services will be opened until the load decreases, and then service will decrease the logging services. Like waiting to pay at the grocery store, when the lines get too long at one cashier, another cashier opens, and people are more evenly distributed until the rush is over, the extra cashier can close again.

A load balancer such as **AWS Elastic Load Balancing** can be used to distribute logging requests across the login servers equally. This is useful when there are too many requests that may overwhelm or slow down SQS. Once the load dies down, the service can go back to using just the SQS service.

Elastic IP addresses are useful when an external client needs to access information over the cloud to a Web service with a VPC. In a scenario where there is no Elastic IP address, the client would lose connectivity if the web service went down and would have to wait to propose a new IP address with the backup server. An Elastic IP decouples the IP address from one server ID allowing it to be used and multiple servers within AWS. The client talks to the application regardless of the server it is on with an elastic IP address.

NOTE:

You can find more information on this topic at the following website links.

https://docs.aws.amazon.com/whitepapers/latest/aws-overview-security-processes/amazon-simple-queue-service-amazon-sqs-security.html

https://docs.aws.amazon.com/elasticloadbalancing/

https://docs.aws.amazon.com/AWSEC2/latest/UserGuide/e
lastic-ip-addresses-eip.html

https://docs.aws.amazon.com/route53/

Determining Resilient Architectures Overview

The best way to determine resilient architecture design for an AWS
environment is to keep the following points in mind:

- Make the use of AWS managed services a preference.

- There is a difference between fault tolerance and high
  availability.

    - Fault tolerance—means that a service can keep
      adding value and operating under certain failures or
      events. The system has no loss of service by hiding
      its failures from the end-users.

    - High availability—means that the service is always
      available and will failover in the event of a failure.

- Always design around the premise that everything will fail
  eventually.

- Don't ever rely on only a single Availability Zone. Services should be able to span at least two Availability Zones to offer resilience.

Domain 1 Practice Test Questions

The following are a few practice exam questions to help test your knowledge. To help you learn how to read the important parts of the questions they have been highlighted in bold text.

Kindly note that all test questions were sourced from AWS (Exam Readiness: AWS Certified Solutions Architect, n.d.). Please see the section under **Chapter 7** for answers to the following.

Practice Exam

Question 1:
A client is running a **database** on an **EC2 instance,** and the database software backup feature needs **block storage**.

Based on the information above, what storage option would you recommend that would be the **lowest cost option** for the backed up data?

Choose one out of four.

A. Amazon S3

B. EBS Cold HDD Volume

C. Amazon Glacier

D. EBS Throughput Optimized HDD Volume

Question 2:

If a customer was looking to implement **loosely coupled architectures,** which of the following AWS services would facilitate this? (Select two).

Choose two out of five.

A. AWS CloudFront

B. Amazon Elastic MapReduce

C. Amazon Simple Queue Service

D. AWS CloudTrail

E. Elastic Load Balancing

Question 3:

A client has a web service with a performance SLA that requires 99% response to requests in <1 second. **Distributing requests over four instances meets performance requirements** under normal to heavy operations.

Based on the information above, if an Availability Zone became unreachable, what architecture would ensure **cost-efficient high availability**?

Choose one out of four.

A. Deploy the service on eight servers across two Availability Zones.

B. Deploy the service on two servers across a single Availability Zone.

C. Deploy the service on four servers across a single Availability Zone.

D. Deploy the service on four servers across two Availability Zones.

Question 4:

How would you use CloudFormation to deploy Linux EC2 instances in two different regions using the same base Amazon Machine Image (AMI)?

Choose one out of four.

A. Use Snapshots of the AMI.

B. Use mappings to specify the base AMI since AMI IDs are different in each region.

C. Use two different CloudFormation templates since CloudFormation templates are region-specific.

D. AMI IDs are identical across regions.

Question 5:

How would you go about accessing print statements from Lambda?

Choose one out of four.

A. CloudWatch Logs

B. Print statements are ignored in Lambda

C. SSH into Lambda and look at system logs

D. Amazon S3 is where Lambda writes all output to

Chapter 3

Design High Performant Architectures

This chapter will cover the best practices for designing performant architectures. At the end of the chapter, there will be a set of practice test questions to give an idea of what the questions will be like in this section of the exam.

Design Performant Architectures Best Practices

The following are the best practices for designing performant AWS architectures.

Storage and Databases

Storage

When choosing storage service based on performance, you should look at solutions such as **EBS** with a few storage solutions to choose from (see Chapter 1 for the different volume/drive specifications).

When looking at choosing EBS as an option, one must first decide if **SSD** or **HDD** better fits the environment. Once that decision has been made it will need to be narrowed down further to choose the drive based on the required type of performance.

Another way to improve performance is by using **Amazon S3** to load all static content from any web server(s). Once static content is taken off a web server, it will improve the server performance as resources will not have to be allocated to the static content. The web server is freed up to deal with dynamic content.

By creating a bucket in one of the AWS Regions, content such as videos, documents, and photos can be uploaded to Amazon S3.

You can find more information on how to upload content to Amazon S3 at the following link:

> https://docs.aws.amazon.com/AmazonS3/latest/user-guide/upload-objects.html

Amazon S3 objects are assigned a URL that is based on the name of the Bucket. It should be noted that Bucket names are unique, and once a bucket name has been created, it cannot be used anywhere else in the world, similar to that of a domain name.

There are different payment structures and storage classes for Amazon S3:

- Amazon S3 Standard Access is the best for general purpose usage.

- Amazon S3 Standard Infrequent Access (IA) gives a lower cost per GB of storage but has a higher charge for GET, PUT, COPY, and POST requests. It also has a minimum 30-day storage requirement.

One of Amazon S3 best features is that lifecycle policies can be set to move files to the Amazon S3 infrequent use and eventually to a service like Glacier for archiving and eventually deleted if the data permits it.

Database

Amazon offers many database solutions such as:

- Relational database service—Using **Amazon RDS**

  - RDS is designed to offer a managed relational database.

  - RDS offers high durability for complex transactions or queries.

  - It can only have a single worker node.

  - It should not be used for sharding or RDBMS customization.

  - It cannot be used for read/writes that exceed 150k write per second.

- The RDS master database can be scaled up and this can be done by using a bigger RDS instance.

- The RDS master database can also be scaled up by using RDS Read Replicas.

  - RDS Read Replicas are supported by MySQL, Postgres, Aurora, and MariaDB

  - RDS Read Replicas work by distributing read requests to the Read Replicas which takes the load off the RDS Master database

- You can find more information on RDs at the following links.

https://docs.aws.amazon.com/AmazonRDS/latest/UserGuide/Welcome.html

https://docs.aws.amazon.com/AmazonRDS/latest/UserGuide/CHAP_GettingStarted.html

- Managed no sequel database—Using **Amazon DynamoDB**

  - For high read rates or throughput DynamoDB is the best solution.

  - Scaling horizontally by adding more servers so it can offer limitless storage.

- Automatic Sharding of data and splits it across servers.

- DynamoDB uses throughput capacity requirements (read/write) to allocate resources.

- It is easy to set up and use.

- DynamoDB grows as the database expands, so the size does not have to be set.

- DynamoDB throughput will, however, need to be specific; this is how many reads and writes per second that are required. These are the Read capacity unit (RCU) and the Write capacity unit (WRU).

  - RCU = 1 strongly consistent read per second for an item of up to 4 kb in size.

  - RCU = 2 eventually consistent reads per second for an item of up to 4 kb in size.

  - WRU = 1 write per second for an item of up to 1 kb in size.

- You can find more information on Amazon DynamoDB at the following link.

https://docs.aws.amazon.com/dynamodb/

- Data Warehousing—Using **Amazon Redshift**

  o Redshift offers a sequel interface

  o Redshift if useful for analytical queries

  o Redshift if handy for computing aggregate numbers across an entire table.

  o You can find out more about Amazon Redshift at the following link(s).

  https://docs.aws.amazon.com/redshift/index.html

Caching

For improved application performance without having to rewrite or redesign a programs core logic.

Caching can be performed at different levels, such as:

Web Level

For web level caching, AWS offers **CloudFront,** which is a **content delivery network (CDN)**. CloudFront caches static content at an edge location that is closer to the system's users. This allows for faster application access time as the request does not have to go all the way back to the Amazon S3 servers.

When a user requests data that is not in the cache, the system will collect it from the Amazon S3 bucket, and that date will automatically be stored in the nearest location cache. The next time it is requested, the data will be retrieved from the cache.

More information and documentation on Amazon CloudFront can be found at the following link:

https://docs.aws.amazon.com/cloudfront/index.html

Application and Database Levels

Amazon offers **ElastiCache** to use between the database front end and database back end. The cache will collect items that are continuously requested of the master database to free up the processing power of the database and make retrieval times on the front end faster.

ElastiCache offers two types of caching options which it will set up for you:

- **Memcached**

    - Horizontal scaling is easy and can be done with Auto Discovery.

    - It allows for multithreading.

    - Memcached is a low maintenance option.

- **Redis**

    o   Offers read replicas or failover.

    o   It is a more sophisticated caching option of the two.

    o   It offers support for data structures.

    o   Has pub/sub messaging.

For more information on ElastiCache and its options, you can go to the following link(s).

https://docs.aws.amazon.com/elasticache/index.html

https://aws.amazon.com/elasticache/memcached/

https://aws.amazon.com/elasticache/redis/resources/

Solutions Designed for Scalability and Elasticity

In a well-architected design, no matter the content or how much traffic an application receives, it should be easy to scale them. If the traffic grows, the system should be able to scale up, and if it drops off, it should be able to scale down, which substantially improves the overall performance.

There are two types of AWS scaling:

- Horizontal scaling (scales in and out)

    o This is when the system grows depending on the number of instances required.

    o The system will add or remove instances as or when required.

- Vertical scaling (scales up and down)

    o This is when the system will replace the specifications of an instance.

    o This is used to allocate specifications such as more memory or more CPU.

Auto Scaling is the easiest way to scale instances as it can be launched across availability zones, can launch and terminate instances as or when needed. It can also register new instances with load balancers automatically.

Auto Scaling works in conjunction with an AWS monitoring service called **CloudWatch**. CloudWatch can be configured with certain instance thresholds that can be triggered when an instance exceeds the set parameters. These alarms will set the **Auto Scaling Policies** into action. These policies will determine the number of instances that need to be launched and what kind of instances to launch.

To learn how to correctly configure both CloudWatch and Auto Scaling, you can find more information at the following links.

https://docs.aws.amazon.com/autoscaling/index.html

https://aws.amazon.com/autoscaling/

https://docs.aws.amazon.com/cloudwatch/index.html

https://aws.amazon.com/cloudwatch/getting-started/

Determining High Performant Architectures

The best way to determine high performant architecture design for an AWS environment is to keep the following points in mind:

- Amazon S3 is the best storage solution for data that is unstructured.

- Always determine the database type and instance that is best for the required performance and workload.

- If there is a large workload that is constantly causing workflow blockages or failures, use caching. Caching can strategically improve system performance.

- Use Auto Scaling for the customers' advantage by knowing when and why to use the service.

Domain 2 Practice Test Questions

The following are a few practice exam questions to help test your knowledge.

Kindly note that all test questions were sourced from AWS (Exam Readiness: AWS Certified Solutions Architect, n.d.).

Please see the section under **Chapter 7** for the answers.

Practice Exam

Question 1:
From the list below, identify which features below to EBS.

Choose two out of four.

    A. Amazon EBS volume can be encrypted.

    B. Data stored on EBS is automatically replicated within an Availability Zone

    C. Data on Amazon EBS volumes is lost when the attached instance is stopped

    D. Amazon EBS data is automatically backed up to tape

Question 2:

For non-relational databases which is the best AWS Service:

Choose one out of four.

A. Amazon Glacier

B. Amazon DynamoDB

C. Amazon Redshift

D. Amazon RDS

Question 3:

Amazon ElastiCache supports which of the following cache engines?

Choose two out of four.

A. Memcached

B. Couchbase

C. MySQL

D. Redis

Question 4:

To launch a fully configured instantly, what is the template that Auto Scaling would use?

Choose one out of four.

    A. User data

    B. Launch configuration

    C. Key pair

    D. Instance type

Question 5:

Of the options below, which are characteristics of the AWS Auto Scaling Service?

Choose two out of six.

    A. Collects and tracks metrics and sets alarms

    B. Delivers push notifications

    C. Sends traffic to healthy instances

    D. Enforces a minimum number of running Amazon EC2 instances

E. Responds to changing conditions by adding or terminating Amazon EC2 instances.

F. Launches instances from a specified Amazon Machine Image (AMI).

Chapter 4

Design Secure Applications and Architectures

Creating well-designed architectures requires the architecture to be efficient, resilient, high performing, and also secure. This chapter looks at creating secure architectures and applications in line with Domain 3 for the SAA-CO2 exams.

Determining Secure Applications and Architectures Best Practices

The following are some best practices for designing secure applications and architectures for an AWS environment:

- **Secure Application Tier**—A cloud solutions architect will need to know how to secure application tiers.

- **Secure Data**—A cloud solutions architect will need to know how to secure the system's data.

- **Defining the Networking Infrastructure**—A cloud solutions architect will need to understand how to define the networking infrastructure for a single VPC and how to secure the networking infrastructure.

Understanding AWS Security

AWS security is one that is shared between the customer and AWS. In order to successfully implement a secure AWS system, the student will need to understand the following AWS security principles and concepts:

- **Shared responsibility model** (protecting the infrastructure)
  - AWS is responsible for the security of the cloud, which includes:
    - AWS Global Infrastructure:
      - Availability zones
      - Regions
      - Edge locations
    - AWS Foundation Services:
      - AWS Compute
      - AWS Storage solutions
      - AWS Databases
      - Networking

- The customer is responsible for the security in the cloud, which includes:

    - Customer content

    - Identity and access management

    - Platform and applications

    - Network traffic protection

    - Server-side data encryption

    - Client-side data encryptions

- **Principle of least privilege** (protecting resources)

    - The principle of least privilege is for managed services such granted access or privileges to users who need to perform specific tasks.

    - Granting access can either limit a user's privilege to just being able to modify certain instances, or being able to modify and delete certain instances, for example. Some users may have full access, and so on.

    - **AWS IAM** service is used to:

- Centrally manage users and their rights within the AWS environment.

- Create users, roles and policies, and groups.

  - **Users**—Users are individuals who are granted permission to access the AWS environment. Permissions for each user are set as a policy, individually assigned, or group access.

  - **Groups**—Groups are set up for various resource rights assignments.

  - **Roles**—Roles are temporary IDs that have various permissions attached to them usually used for external users. Like a guest-pass into a building that only allows access to certain areas of the building. These permissions are set as policies.

  - **Policies**—Policies are set up per resource and contain permissions for the resource. For instance, a policy set for a certain printer may state that

Policy 1 users can only print in black and white. Policy 2 users can use color but are limited to 6 pages per user per month. Policies can be assigned to a user, a group, or a role.

- Allocates permissions to AWS users to grant them access to or restrict their access to various AWS resources or various applications running on the system.

- IAM uses **SAML identity federation** to interface with AWS Directory and Microsoft Active Directory.

- **Identities** (protecting resources)

  ○ Many different forms of identities can be created in a customer's AWS environment, and these include:

    - IAM users for creating user IDs within an Amazon account.

    - Roles are temporary IDs created within an Amazon account and are used by external users, EC2 instances, and Lambdas.

- Federation identities use SAML to connect to identities that have been created in applications such as Active Directory but have been assigned right to AWS through an IAM role.

- Web Identity Federation identities—Uses Security Token Service (STS) allows roles to be assigned to users with certain Open IDs from various open-source providers. It also allows roles to be assigned to users who have an Amazon.com ID.

For more information on understanding AWS Security the following links have a lot of valuable information.

https://d0.awsstatic.com/whitepapers/aws-security-whitepaper.pdf

https://docs.aws.amazon.com/iam/index.html

https://docs.aws.amazon.com/STS/latest/APIReference/welcome.html

https://d1.awsstatic.com/whitepapers/Security/AWS_Security_Best_Practices.pdf

Securing Infrastructure in the Cloud using Amazon Virtual Private Cloud (VPC)

A client's network infrastructure in the cloud can be protected by using Virtual Private Cloud (VPC).

Virtual Private Cloud (VPC)

- VPCs are divided into subnetworks of private IP addresses called subnets.

- Security groups and access control lists are used to determine communication access between specific sources.

- To allow data to flow in and out of the VPC NAT gateways, internet gateways, and virtual private gateways get set up.

- Routing (routes/routing table) is set up to determine the traffic flow/direction.

For allowing access or restricting access in a VPC, the two main resources are:

- Network Access Control List (ACL)

   ○ Operate at the subnet level

   ○ Rules—Explicit allow or deny protocols

   ○ State—Stateless

- o Access type—A port, protocol, or source IP needs to be specified

- o Associations—Single VPC

- o Only supports VPC

- o Application—Applied to subnets

- Security Groups

  - o Operate at the instance or network interface level

  - o Rules—Explicit allow only

  - o State—Stateful

  - o Access type—A port, protocol, or source IP needs to be specified

  - o Associations—Single VPC

  - o Supports EC2 Classic and VPC

  - o Application—Applied to ENIs

Links to documentation for more information on VPC:

https://docs.aws.amazon.com/vpc/latest/userguide/what-is-amazon-vpc.html

https://docs.aws.amazon.com/vpc/latest/userguide/vpc-ug.pdf

https://aws.amazon.com/blogs/security/tag/bastion-host/

Securing Applications in an AWS Environment

Security groups can be used to separate access to application tiers in an AWS environment.

Securing Data in an AWS Environment

To secure data in AWS you need to look at data in two entities.

Data in Transit

Data in transit is data that moves into or out of AWS or within AWS.

To create a secure environment for data in transit for an AWS environment should be done through:

- For transferring data through AWS infrastructure

  o Moving data over the web, it is best to use SSL.

  o Moving data between AWS corporate data centers, it is best to use a VPN for IPsec.

  o For AWS Direct Connect, it is best to use IPsec.

○ AWS import or export services can be used with AWS Snowball or AWS Snowmobile.

○ All the devices mentioned above are designed to keep the data encrypted and are tamper-proof.

- For sending data to AWS API

○ When data is sent from AWS to AWS API, it is done so through HTTPS/SSL as a default setting.

Data at Rest

Data at rest is data that is stored using either an AWS service or other service running inside of AWS. Some AWS services that can be applied to data at rest are Amazon EBS or Amazon S3.

The best solution for keeping data secure on AWS is to store it on an AWS service such as Amazon S3, which is set to private for each customer by default. The service being private automatically requires authentication with a user id that has been granted specific access to data.

Amazon S3 can be accessed over HTTP or HTTPS, it supports both Access List Control (ACL) and policies, and an audit of access to all objects.

To lockdown data at rest in the AWS environment, AWS offers a few options to do this for:

- Client-side encryption

    - Customer managed master encryption keys (CSE-C)

    - KMS managed master encryption keys (CES0-KMS)

- Server-side encryption

    - Customer-provided keys (SSE-C)

    - Amazon S3-managed keys (SSE-S3)

    - KMS-managed keys (SSE-KMS)

Security Key Management

To securely manage and store security keys, AWS offers a few solutions, which include:

- Key Management Services (KMS)

    - AWS KMS can be integrated with many other AWS services:

        - EBS

        - S3

        - RDS

- EMR

- WorkMail

- Elastic Transcoder

- Redshift

  o Customer software-based

  o If requested encryption is done for the customer

- AWS CloudHSM

  o CloudHSM is a dedicated appliance for managing security keys.

  o CloudHSM offers FIPS 140-2 compliance

  o Hardware-based

The following links are filled with information on securing data within an AWS environment.

https://aws.amazon.com/blogs/database/best-practices-for-securing-sensitive-data-in-aws-data-stores/

https://aws.amazon.com/compliance/data-privacy-faq/

https://docs.aws.amazon.com/whitepapers/latest/building-data-lakes/securing-protecting-managing-data.html

https://docs.aws.amazon.com/kms/

https://docs.aws.amazon.com/cloudhsm/latest/userguide/introduction.html

Determining Security

The best way to determine the security architecture is to keep the following points in mind when designing an AWS solution:

- Ensure the root user is locked down.

- Use IAM Roles as a preference over access keys.

- Keep in mind that Security groups have only explicit allow access.

- Network access control lists (ACL) have explicit allow and explicit deny.

Domain 3 Practice Test Questions

The following are a few practice exam questions to help test your knowledge.

Kindly note that all test questions were sourced from AWS (Exam Readiness: AWS Certified Solutions Architect, n.d.).

Please see the section under **Chapter 7** for the answers.

Practice Exam

Question 1:

An administrator had access to the root user, and they had a personal IAM administrator account. With these accounts, the administrator was able to generate IAM users and keys. The administrator left the company for good today. To protect the AWS infrastructure, what should be done right away?

Choose three out of six.

    A. Delete all IAM users.

    B. Relaunch all EC2 instances with new roles.

    C. Rotate keys and change passwords for IAM users.

    D. Put an IP restriction on root user logins.

    E. Delete the administrator in question IAM user.

    F. Change the password and add MFA to the root user.

Question 2:

From the actions below, which ones can be controlled by **IAM policies**?

Choose three out of five.

    A. Creating an Amazon S3 bucket

    B. Logging into .NET applications

    C. Creating tables in a MySQL RDS database

    D. Configuring a VPC security group

    E. Creating an Oracle RDS database

Chapter 5

Design Cost-Optimized Architectures

This chapter looks at designing cost-optimized architectures by determining the best solutions for cost-optimized storage and compute designs.

Best Practices for Cost-Optimized Architectures

There are three types of payment structures for cost-optimization in AWS, and these include:

- **Pay as you go**

  - Only pay for what you use

- **Pay less when you reserve service in advance**

  - Reserving instances in advance will give the customer discounts

  - Reserved instances are offered higher priority and capacity

- **Pay less per unit by using more**

  - Because AWS prices are tiered there are volume discounts

o   The more usage, the cheaper the services

In AWS, there are three fundamental characteristics that a customer pays for, and these include:

Compute
Amazon EC2 costing is based on:

- Machine configuration

- Machine purchase type

- Number of instances

- Load balancing

- Auto Scaling

- Detailed monitoring

- Elastic IP monitoring

- Operating systems

- Software packages

- Hours of server time usage —How many hours and instances ran for.

Saving with EC2

- Use reserved instances which can give up to 75% discount. There are three different types of Reserved Instances (RIs):

    - Standard Reserved Instances

    - Convertible Reserved Instances

    - Scheduled Reserved Instances

- Spot instances a spare compute instance within the cloud that is sold at a discount of up to 45%.

    - These are dynamically priced instances based on the spot price of the market.

    - There is a risk using these instances as you could lose the instance if the price goes above the price of your bed.

    - There are ways around this risk by using services such as:

        - Hibernate, which will put the instance to sleep while the price is above the price of your bed.

        - Spot Blocks which block off up to six hours on the spot market.

Serverless Architectures

One of the best ways to ensure cost-optimized AWS architectures is with serverless architectures, which means that the customer does not pay for any idle time of an EC2 instance.

Serverless architecture can reduce the compute spend:

- Amazon S3 can be used for static files in an AWS serverless environment.

- AWS Lambda can use DynamoDB for storing state and the Amazon API Gateway to attach to Lambda to be called from any browser over the web.

- CloudFront can be used by caching data on it as there are no costs when data is transferred between CloudFront and Amazon S3.

Storage

The different storage services offered by AWS each have different pricing structures and considerations to be taken into account before implementing them.

Amazon S3

The main consideration for creating a cost-optimized storage solution in AWS S3 pricing is:

- Storage Class

- Storage Amount

- Number of Requests

- Data Transfer Amount

Amazon S3 pricing can be broken down into (pricing may differ according to AWS pricing update which can be referenced on the AWS website pricing pages):

- Standard storage

  - First 50TB/ Month = $0.023 per GB

  - Next 450TB/Month = $0.022 per GB

  - Over 500TB/Month = $0.021 per GB

- Standard infrequent access

  - All storage = $0.0125 per GB

- Amazon Glacier

  - All storage = $0.004 per GB

Amazon EBS
The main consideration for creating a cost-optimized storage solution in Amazon EBS pricing are:

- To move the snapshots to other regions, there is a cost for data transfer.

- Storage of snapshots and the frequency and length of storage for the snapshots.

- Amount of snapshots.

- The types of volumes the customer provisions.

- Input/Output operations per second (IOPS) the customer has requested.

Amazon EBS pricing can be broken down into (pricing may differ according to AWS pricing update which can be referenced on the AWS website pricing pages):

- Hard Disk Drives (HDD)

  - The cheaper option for EBS storage

  - HDD have lower IOPS than SSD drives

  - HDD drives come in useful for sequential data

- Solid State Drives (SSD)

  - The more expensive option for EBS storage

  - SSD drives offer higher IOPS

  - SSD driver is more useful for random access

Determining Cost Optimization

The best way to determine cost optimization is to keep the following points in mind when designing an AWS solution:

- Determine costs per workload based on the instance type for the most cost-effective EC2 pricing model.

- Find the most cost-effective data storage class and service.

- Money is being wasted if there is any unused CPU time.

- If an instance needs to be run at a certain time, it is always more cost-effective to reserve it.

Domain 4 Practice Test Questions

The following are a few practice exam questions to help test your knowledge. Kindly note that all test questions were sourced from AWS (Exam Readiness: AWS Certified Solutions Architect, n.d.). Please see the section under **Chapter 7** for the answers.

Practice Exam

Question 1:

A customer needs a file, such as a PDF file made available to be publicly downloadable. The PDF file is going to be downloaded by customers using their browsers. The PDF file will be downloaded in this manner millions of times. From the options below, which will be the most cost-effective for the customer?

Choose one out of four.

A. Store the file in Glacier

B. Store the file in EFS

C. Store the file in S3 Standard

D. Store the file in S3 Standard-IA

Chapter 6

AWS Certified Solutions Architect Associate Test Questions

Read each question carefully and make sure you understand it before answering and moving on to the next one. An unanswered question is marked as incorrect and will negatively affect your overall score.

Here are 33 practice sample exam questions to help test your knowledge. Kindly note that these questions are sourced from ExamTopics (2020) and AWS Training and Certification (n.d.). Please see the corresponding section under **Chapter 7** for the answers.

Question 1:
A mobile phone application runs statistical articles from individual files in an Amazon S3 bucket. There are articles older than 40 days that are no longer needed for the application and articles over 30 days old that are hardly ever read. These articles are no longer needed to be visible through the mobile application but must be archived for historical data purposes.

From the list below, select the cost-effective solution that <u>best</u> meets these requirements.

Choose one out of four.

A. For files older than 30 days, create lifecycle rules to move these files to Amazon S3 Standard Infrequent Access and use Amazon Glacier to move files older than 40 days to.

B. For files older than 30 days, create a Lambda function to move them to Amazon Glacier and move files older than 40 days to Amazon EBS.

C. Create a Lambda function that moves files to Amazon EBS that are older than 30 days and move files to Amazon Glacier that are older than 40 days.

D. For files older than 30 days, create lifecycle rules to move these files to Amazon Glacier and use Amazon S3 Standard Infrequent Access to move files older than 40 days to.

Question 2:

A company is launching an application that it expects to be very popular. The company needs a database that can scale with the rest of the application. The schema will change frequently. The application cannot afford any downtime for database changes.

Which AWS service allows the company to achieve these objectives?

Choose one out of four.

    A. Amazon Aurora

    B. Amazon RDS MySQL

    C. Amazon Redshift

    D. Amazon DynamoDB

Question 3:

A Solutions Architect is designing a new social media application. The application must provide a secure method for uploading profile photos. Each user should be able to upload a profile photo into a shared storage location for one week after their profile is created.

Which approach will meet all of these requirements?

Choose one out of four.

    A. Use Amazon S3 with the default private access policy and generate pre-signed URLs each time a new site profile is created.

B. Use Amazon CloudFront with AWS CloudTrail for auditing the specific times when profile photos are uploaded.

C. Use Amazon EBS volumes with IAM policies restricting user access to specific time periods.

D. Use Amazon Kinesis with AWS CloudTrail for auditing the specific times when profile photos are uploaded.

Question 4:

A Solutions Architect needs to build a resilient data warehouse using Amazon Redshift. The Architect needs to rebuild the Redshift cluster in another region.

Which approach can the Architect take to address this requirement?

Choose one out of four.

A. Modify the Redshift cluster and configure the backup and specify the Amazon S3 bucket in the other region.

B. Modify the Redshift cluster and configure cross-region snapshots to the other region.

C. Modify the Redshift cluster to take snapshots of the Amazon EBS volumes each day, sharing those snapshots with the other region.

D. Modify the Redshift cluster to use AWS Snowball in export mode with data delivered to the other region.

Question 5:

A Solutions Architect is designing the architecture for a new three-tier web-based e-commerce site that must be available 24/7. Requests are expected to range from 100 to 10,000 each minute. Usage can vary depending on the time of day, holidays, and promotions. The design should be able to handle these volumes, with the ability to handle higher volumes if necessary.

How should the Architect design the architecture to ensure the web tier is cost-optimized and can handle the expected traffic?

Choose two out of five.

A. Use Amazon Route 53 to route traffic to the correct region.

B. Store all static files in a multi-AZ Amazon Aurora database.

C. Create a CloudFront distribution pointing to static content in Amazon S3.

D. Launch Amazon EC2 instances in an Auto Scaling group behind an ELB.

E. Use Amazon S3 multipart uploads to improve upload times.

Question 6:

An e-commerce application is hosted in AWS. The last time a new product was launched, the application experienced a performance issue due to an enormous spike in traffic. Management decided that capacity must be doubled the week after the product is launched.

Which is the <u>most</u> efficient way for management to ensure that capacity requirements are met?

Choose one out of four.

A. Add a Scheduled Scaling action

B. Add a Dynamic Scaling policy

C. Add a Step Scaling policy

D. Add Amazon EC2 Spot instances

Question 7:

A Solutions Architect is designing a solution that includes a managed VPN connection.

To monitor whether the VPN connection is up or down, the Architect should use:

Choose one out of four.

A. The CloudWatch TunnelState Metric.

B. An external service to ping the VPN endpoint from outside the VPC.

C. An AWS Lambda function that parses the VPN connection logs.

D. AWS CloudTrail to monitor the endpoint.

Question 8:

A Solutions Architect is designing a log-processing solution that requires storage that supports up to 500 MB/s throughput. The data is sequentially accessed by an Amazon EC2 instance.

Which Amazon storage type satisfies these requirements?

Choose one out of four.

A. EBS Cold HDD (sc1)

B. EBS Provisioned IOPS SSD (io1)

C. EBS General Purpose SSD (gp2)

D. EBS Throughput Optimized HDD (st1)

Question 9:
A Solutions Architect is designing network architecture for an application that has compliance requirements. The application will be hosted on Amazon EC2 instances in a private subnet and will be using Amazon S3 for storing data. The compliance requirements mandate that the data cannot traverse the public Internet.

What is the <u>most</u> secure way to satisfy this requirement?

Choose one out of four.

  A. Use a NAT Instance

  B. Use a VPC endpoint

  C. Use a Virtual Private Gateway

  D. Use a NAT Gateway

Question 10:
A company has a legacy application using a proprietary file system and plans to migrate the application to AWS.

Which storage service should the company use?

Choose one out four.

    A. Amazon DynamoDB

    B. Amazon S3

    C. Amazon EBS

    D. Amazon EFS

Question 11:

A company is launching a static website using the zone apex (mycompany.com). The company wants to use Amazon Route 53 for DNS.

Which steps should the company perform to implement a scalable and cost-effective solution?

Choose two out of five.

    A. Host the website on an Amazon EC2 instance with ELB and Auto Scaling, and map a Route 53 alias record to the ELB endpoint.

    B. Host the website using AWS Elastic Beanstalk, and map a Route 53 alias record to the Beanstalk stack.

C. Host the website on an Amazon EC2 instance, and map a Route 53 alias record to the public IP address of the Amazon EC2 instance.

D. Serve the website from an Amazon S3 bucket, and map a Route 53 alias record to the website endpoint.

E. Create a Route 53 hosted zone, and set the NS records of the domain to use Route 53 name servers.

Question 12:

A Solutions Architect is designing a new application that needs to access data in a different AWS account located within the same region. The data must not be accessed over the Internet.

Which solution will meet these requirements with the <u>lowest</u> cost?

Choose one out of four.

A. Add rules to the security groups in each account.

B. Establish a VPC Peering connection between accounts.

C. Configure Direct Connect in each account.

D. Add a NAT Gateway to the data account.

Question 13:

A Solutions Architect has a multi-layer application running in Amazon VPC. The application has an ELB Classic Load Balancer as the front end in a public subnet, and an Amazon EC2-based reverse proxy that performs content-based routing to two backend Amazon EC2 instances hosted in a private subnet. The Architect sees tremendous traffic growth and is concerned that the reverse proxy and current backend setup will be insufficient.

Which actions should the Architect take to achieve a cost-effective solution that ensures the application automatically scales to meet traffic demand?

Choose two out of five.

A. Replace the Amazon EC2 reverse proxy with an ELB internal Classic Load Balancer.

B. Add Auto Scaling to the Amazon EC2 backend fleet.

C. Add Auto Scaling to the Amazon EC2 reverse proxy layer.

D. Use t2 burstable instance types for the backend fleet.

E. Replace both the frontend and reverse proxy layers with an ELB Application Load Balancer.

Question 14:

A Solutions Architect plans to migrate NAT instances to NAT gateway. The Architect has NAT instances with scripts to manage high availability.

What is the _most_ efficient method to achieve similar high availability with NAT gateway?

Choose one out of four.

  A. Remove source/destination check on NAT instances.

  B. Launch a NAT gateway in each Availability Zone.

  C. Use a mix of NAT instances and NAT gateway.

  D. Add an ELB Application Load Balancer in front of NAT gateway.

Question 15:

A Solutions Architect is designing a web application. The web and application tiers need to access the Internet, but they cannot be accessed from the Internet.

Which of the following steps is required?

Choose one out of four.

A. Attach an Elastic IP address to each Amazon EC2 instance and add a route from the private subnet to the public subnet.

B. Launch a NAT gateway in the public subnet and add a route to it from the private subnet.

C. Launch Amazon EC2 instances in the public subnet and change the security group to allow outbound traffic on port 80.

D. Launch a NAT gateway in the private subnet and deploy a NAT instance in the private subnet.

Question 16:

A Solutions Architect is designing a database solution that must support a high rate of random disk reads and writes. It must provide consistent performance, and requires long-term persistence.

Which storage solution best meets these requirements?

Choose one out of four.

A. An Amazon EBS Provisioned IOPS volume

B. An Amazon EBS General Purpose volume

C. An Amazon EBS Magnetic volume

D. An Amazon EC2 Instance Store

Question 17:

A Solutions Architect is designing a Lambda function that calls an API to list all running Amazon RDS instances.

How should the request be authorized?

Choose one out four.

    A. Create an IAM access and secret key, and store it in the Lambda function.

    B. Create an IAM role to the Lambda function with permissions to list all Amazon RDS instances.

    C. Create an IAM role to Amazon RDS with permissions to list all Amazon RDS instances.

    D. Create an IAM access and secret key, and store it in an encrypted RDS database.

Question 18:

An interactive, dynamic website runs on Amazon EC2 instances in a single subnet behind an ELB Classic Load Balancer.

Which design changes will make the site more highly available?

Choose one out four.

A. Move some Amazon EC2 instances to a subnet in a different way.

B. Move the website to Amazon S3.

C. Change the ELB to an Application Load Balancer.

D. Move some Amazon EC2 instances to a subnet in the same Availability Zone.

Question 19:

A Solutions Architect is about to deploy an API on multiple EC2 instances in an Auto Scaling group behind an ELB. The support team has the following operational requirements:

1. They get an alert when the requests per second go over 50,000.

2. They get an alert when latency goes over 5 seconds.

3. They can validate how many times a day users call the API requesting highly-sensitive data.

Which combination of steps does the Architect need to take to satisfy these operational requirements?

Choose two out five.

A. Ensure that CloudTrail is enabled.

B. Create a custom CloudWatch metric to monitor the API for data access.

C. Configure CloudWatch alarms for any metrics the support team requires.

D. Ensure that detailed monitoring for the EC2 instances is enabled.

E. Create an application to export and save CloudWatch metrics for longer-term trending analysis.

Question 20:

A Solutions Architect is designing a web application that is running on an Amazon EC2 instance. The application stores data in DynamoDB. The Architect needs to secure access to the DynamoDB table.

What combination of steps does AWS recommend to achieve secure authorization?

Choose two out of five.

A. Store an access key on the Amazon EC2 instance with rights to the DynamoDB table.

B. Attach an IAM user to the Amazon EC2 instance.

C. Create an IAM role with permissions to write to the DynamoDB table.

D. Attach an IAM role to the Amazon EC2 instance.

E. Attach an IAM policy to the Amazon EC2 instance.

Question 21:

A Solutions Architect is designing the storage layer for a production relational database. The database will run on Amazon EC2. The database is accessed by an application that performs intensive reads and writes, so the database requires the lowest random I/O latency.

Which data storage method fulfills the above requirements?

Choose one out of four.

A. Store data in a filesystem backed by Amazon Elastic File System (EFS).

B. Store data in Amazon S3 and use a third-party solution to expose Amazon S3 as a filesystem to the database server.

C. Store data in Amazon DynamoDB and emulate relational database semantics.

D. Stripe data across multiple Amazon EBS volumes using RAID 0.

Question 22:

A web application stores all data in an Amazon RDS Aurora database instance. A Solutions Architect wants to provide access to the data for a detailed report for the Marketing team but is concerned that the additional load on the database will affect the performance of the web application.

How can the report be created without affecting the performance of the application?

Choose one out of four.

    A. Create a read replica of the database.

    B. Provision of a new RDS instance as a secondary master.

    C. Configure the database to be in multiple regions.

    D. Increase the number of provisioned storage IOPS.

Question 23:

A company hosts a popular web application. The web application connects to a database running in a private VPC subnet. The web servers must be accessible only to customers on an SSL connection. The RDS MySQL database server must be accessible only from the web servers.

How should the Architect design a solution to meet the requirements without impacting running applications?

Choose one out of four.

A. Create a network ACL on the web server's subnet, and allow HTTPS inbound and MySQL outbound. Place both database and web servers on the same subnet.

B. Open an HTTPS port on the security group for web servers and set the source to 0.0.0.0/0. Open the MySQL port on the database security group and attach it to the MySQL instance. Set the source to Web Server Security Group.

C. Create a network ACL on the web server's subnet, and allow HTTPS inbound, and specify the source as 0.0.0.0/0. Create a network ACL on a database subnet, allow MySQL port inbound for web servers, and deny all outbound traffic.

D. Open the MySQL port on the security group for web servers and set the source to 0.0.0.0/0. Open the HTTPS port on the database security group and attach it to the MySQL instance. Set the source to Web Server Security Group.

Question 24:

A company's website receives 50,000 requests each second, and the company wants to use multiple applications to analyze the navigation patterns of the users on their website so that the experience can be personalized.

What can a Solutions Architect use to collect page clicks for the website and process them sequentially for each user?

Choose one out four.

    A. Amazon Kinesis Stream

    B. Amazon SQS standard queue

    C. Amazon SQS FIFO queue

    D. AWS CloudTrail trail

Question 25:

A company hosts a two-tier application that consists of a publicly accessible web server that communicates with a private database. Only HTTPS port 443 traffic to the web server must be allowed from the Internet.

Which of the following options will achieve these requirements?

Choose two out of five.

A. Security group rule that allows inbound Internet traffic for port 443.

B. Security group rule that denies all inbound Internet traffic except port 443.

C. Network ACL rule that allows port 443 inbound and all ports outbound for Internet traffic.

D. Security group rule that allows Internet traffic for port 443 in both inbound and outbound.

E. Network ACL rule that allows port 443 for both inbound and outbound for all Internet traffic.

Question 26:

A development team is building an application with front-end and back-end application tiers. Each tier consists of Amazon EC2 instances behind an ELB Classic Load Balancer. The instances run in Auto Scaling groups across multiple Availability Zones. The network team has allocated the 10.0.0.0/24 address space for this application. Only the front-end load balancer should be exposed to the Internet. There are concerns about the limited size of the address space and the ability of each tier to scale.

What should the VPC subnet design be in each Availability Zone?

Choose one out of four.

A. One public subnet for the load balancer tier, one public subnet for the front-end tier, and one private subnet for the backend tier.

B. One shared public subnet for all tiers of the application.

C. One public subnet for the load balancer tier and one shared private subnet for the application tiers.

D. One shared private subnet for all tiers of the application.

Question 27:

Legacy applications currently send messages through a single Amazon EC2 instance, which then routes the messages to the appropriate destinations. The Amazon EC2 instance is a bottleneck and single point of failure, so the company would like to address these issues.

Which services could address this architectural use case?

Choose two out of five.

A. Amazon SNS

B. AWS STS

C. Amazon SQS

D. Amazon Route 53

E. AWS Glue

Question 28:

A Solutions Architect needs to allow developers to have SSH connectivity to web servers. The requirements are as follows:

1. Limit access to users' origination from the corporate network.

2. Web servers cannot have SSH access directly from the Internet.

3. Web servers reside in a private subnet.

Which combination of steps must the Architect complete to meet these requirements?

Choose two out of five.

A. Create a bastion host that authenticates users against the corporate directory.

B. Create a bastion host with security group rules that only allow traffic from the corporate network.

C. Attach an IAM role to the bastion host with relevant permissions.

D. Configure the web servers' security group to allow SSH traffic from a bastion host.

E. Deny all SSH traffic from the corporate network in the inbound network ACL.

Question 29:

A company is designing a failover strategy in Amazon Route 53 for its resources between two AWS Regions. The company must have the ability to route a user's traffic to the region with the least latency, and if both regions are healthy, Route 53 should route traffic to resources in both regions.

Which strategy should the Solutions Architect recommend?

Choose one out four.

A. Configure active-active failover using Route 53 latency DNS records.

B. Configure active-passive failover using Route 53 latency DNS records.

C. Configure active-active failover using Route 53 failover DNS records.

D. Configure active-passive failover using Route 53 failover DNS records.

Question 30:

A company must collect temperature data from thousands of remote weather devices. The company must also store this data in a data warehouse to run aggregations and visualizations.

Which services will meet these requirements?

Choose two out of five.

    A. Amazon Kinesis Data Firehouse

    B. Amazon SQS

    C. Amazon Redshift

    D. Amazon SNS

    E. Amazon DynamoDB

Question 31:

A company is implementing a data lake solution on Amazon S3. Its security policy mandates that the data stored in Amazon S3 should be encrypted at rest.

Which options can achieve this?

Choose two out of five.

    A. Use SSL to encrypt the data while in transit to Amazon S3

B. Use S3 server-side encryption with customer-provided keys (SSE-C).

C. Use S3 bucket policies to restrict access to the data at rest.

D. Use client-side encryption before ingesting the data to Amazon S3 using encryption keys.

E. Use S3 server-side encryption with an Amazon EC2 key pair.

Question 32:
An online retailer has a series of flash sales occurring every Friday. Sales traffic will increase during the sales only and the platform will handle the increased load.

The platform is a three-tier application. The web tier runs on Amazon EC2 instances behind an Application Load Balancer. Amazon CloudFront is used to reduce web server load, but many requests for dynamic content must go to the web servers.

What should be done to the web tier to reduce costs without impacting performance or reliability?

Choose one out of four.

A. Use Spot Instances.

B. Implement Amazon ElastiCache.

C. Purchase scheduled Reserved Instances.

D. Use T-series instances.

Question 33:

A Solutions Architect is designing the architecture for a web application that will be hosted on AWS. Internet users will access the application using HTTP and HTTPS.

How should the Architect design the traffic control requirements?

Choose one out of four.

A. Use a network ACL to allow outbound ports for HTTP and HTTPS. Deny other traffic for inbound and outbound.

B. Use a network ACL to allow inbound ports for HTTP and HTTPS. Deny other traffic for inbound and outbound.

C. Allow inbound ports for HTTP and HTTPS in the security group used by the web servers.

D. Allow outbound ports for HTTP and HTTPS in the security group used by the web servers.

Chapter 7

AWS Solutions Architect Associate Test Question Answers

Answers are listed per chapter from Chapter 1 through Chapter 12. Kindly note that these answers, as per the questions, are sourced from ExamTopics (2020, July 4) and AWS Training and Certification (n.d.).

Chapter 2: Design Resilient Architectures Test Question Answers

Answer to Question 1:
 A. For files older than 30 days, create lifecycle rules to move these files to Amazon S3 Standard Infrequent Access and use Amazon Glacier to move files older than 40 days.

Answer to Question 2:
 C. Amazon Simple Queue Service

 E. Elastic Load Balancing

Answer to Question 3:
 D. Deploy the service on four servers across two Availability Zones.

Answer to Question 4:

    B. Use mappings to specify the base AMI since AMI IDs are different in each region.

Answer to Question 5:

    A. CloudWatch Logs

Chapter 3: Design High-Performing Architectures Test Question Answers

Answer to Question 1:

    A. Amazon EBS volume can be encrypted.

    B. Data stored on EBS is automatically replicated within an Availability Zone.

Answer to Question 2:

    B. Amazon DynamoDB

Answer to Question 3:

    A. Memcached

    D. Redis

Answer to Question 4:

    B. Launch configuration

Answer to Question 5:

    D. Enforces a minimum number of running Amazon EC2 instances.

    E. Responds to changing conditions by adding or terminating Amazon EC2 instances.

    F. Launches instances from a specified Amazon Machine Image (AMI).

Chapter 4: Design Secure Applications and Architectures Test Question Answers

Answer to Question 1:

    C. Rotate keys and change passwords for IAM users.

    E. Delete the administrator in question IAM user.

    F. Change the password and add MFA to the root user.

Answer to Question 2:

    A. Creating an Amazon S3 bucket

    D. Configuring a VPC security group

    E. Creating an Oracle RDS database

Chapter 5: Design Cost-Optimized Architectures Test Question Answers

Answer to Question 1:

C. Store the file in S3 Standard

Chapter 6: AWS Certified Solutions Architect Associate Test Questions Answers

Answer to Question 1:

A. For files older than 30 days, create lifecycle rules to move these files to Amazon S3 Standard Infrequent Access and use Amazon Glacier to move files older than 40 days to.

Answer to Question 2:

C. Amazon Redshift

Answer to Question 3:

A. Use Amazon S3 with the default private access policy and generate pre-signed URLs each time a new site profile is created.

Answer to Question 4:

C. Modify the Redshift cluster to take snapshots of the Amazon EBS volumes each day, sharing those snapshots with the other region.

Answer to Question 5:

    C. Create a CloudFront distribution pointing to static content in Amazon S3.

    D. Launch Amazon EC2 instances in an Auto Scaling group behind an ELB.

Answer to Question 6:

    B. Add a Dynamic Scaling policy

Answer to Question 7:

    A. the CloudWatch TunnelState Metric

Answer to Question 8:

    D. EBS Throughput Optimized HDD (st1)

Answer to Question 9:

    B. Use a VPC endpoint

Answer to Question 10:

    C. Amazon EBS

Answer to Question 11:

    C. Host the website on an Amazon EC2 instance, and map a Route 53 alias record to the public IP address of the Amazon EC2 instance.

    D. Serve the website from an Amazon S3 bucket, and map a Route 53 alias record to the website endpoint.

Answer to Question 12:

B. Establish a VPC Peering connection between accounts.

Answer to Question 13:

A. Replace the Amazon EC2 reverse proxy with an ELB internal Classic Load Balancer.

B. Add Auto Scaling to the Amazon EC2 backend fleet.

Answer to Question 14:

B. Launch a NAT gateway in each Availability Zone.

Answer to Question 15:

B. Launch a NAT gateway in the public subnet and add a route to it from the private subnet.

Answer to Question 16:

A. An Amazon EBS Provisioned IOPS volume

Answer to Question 17:

C. Create an IAM role to Amazon RDS with permissions to list all Amazon RDS instances.

Answer to Question 18:

A. Move some Amazon EC2 instances to a subnet in a different way.

Answer to Question 19:

    B. Create a custom CloudWatch metric to monitor the API for data access.

    D. Ensure that detailed monitoring for the EC2 instances is enabled.

Answer to Question 20:

    C. Create an IAM role with permissions to write to the DynamoDB table.

    D. Attach an IAM role to the Amazon EC2 instance.

Answer to Question 21:

    D. Stripe data across multiple Amazon EBS volumes using RAID 0.

Answer to Question 22:

    B. Provision a new RDS instance as a secondary master.

Answer to Question 23:

    B. Open an HTTPS port on the security group for web servers and set the source to 0.0.0.0/0. Open the MySQL port on the database security group and attach it to the MySQL instance. Set the source to the Web Server Security Group.

Answer to Question 24:

    A. Amazon Kinesis Stream

Answer to Question 25:

A. Security group rule that allows inbound Internet traffic for port 443.

E. Network ACL rule that allows port 443 for both inbound and outbound for all Internet traffic.

Answer to Question 26:

A. One public subnet for the load balancer tier, one public subnet for the front-end tier, and one private subnet for the backend tier.

Answer to Question 27:

A. Amazon SNS

C. Amazon SQS

Answer to Question 28:

A. Create a bastion host that authenticates users against the corporate directory.

C. Attach an IAM role to the bastion host with relevant permissions.

Answer to Question 29:

A. Configure active-active failover using Route 53 latency DNS records.

Answer to Question 30:

   A. Amazon Kinesis Data Firehouse

   B. Amazon SQS

Answer to Question 31:

   C. Use S3 bucket policies to restrict access to the data at rest.

   E. Use S3 server-side encryption with an Amazon EC2 key pair.

Answer to Question 32:

   C. Purchase scheduled Reserved Instances.

Answer to Question 33:

   C. Allow inbound ports for HTTP and HTTPS in the security group used by the web servers.

Conclusion

The AWS Certified Solutions Architect Associate qualification is a respected and valuable certification. It will benefit any cloud solutions architect working with AWS. This certification offers many opportunities for career advancement in a competitive field. The AWS SAA-CO2 certification gives credibility to an IT professional's AWS cloud computing skills. Employers regard the certification as a testimony to the bearer's abilities.

The AWS Certified Solutions Architect Associate qualification is an associate-level certification and is the entry-level for the more advanced and specialized certifications.

Although the SAA-CO2 is not an easy exam, it is not an impossible one. It will take hard work, dedication, hands-on experience, and commitment to your studies. But you will find your efforts are well worth it. SAA-CO2 validates your knowledge of the AWS core services and shows that you are able to design, maintain, and optimize efficient AWS systems.

For more confidence and an extra bit of help, this guide, you can increase your chances of passing the exam. It will also help to bring your thoughts together and focus on the important parts.

Good luck!

References

Amazon AWS Certified Solutions Architect - Associate Exam Actual Questions. (2020, July 4). ExamTopics. https://www.examtopics.com/exams/amazon/aws-certified-solutions-architect-associate/view/1/

AWS Certified Solutions Architect – Associate. (n.d.). AWS Training and Certification. https://aws.amazon.com/certification/certified-solutions-architect-associate/

AWS Certified Solutions Architect – Associate(SAA-C02) Exam Guide [PDF File]. (n.d.). AWS Training and Certification. https://d1.awsstatic.com/training-and-certification/docs-sa-assoc/AWS-Certified-Solutions-Architect-Associate_Exam-Guide.pdf

AWS Certified Solutions Architect – Associate (SAA-C02)Sample Exam Questions [PDF File]. (n.d.). AWS Training and Certification. https://d1.awsstatic.com/training-and-certification/docs-sa-assoc/AWS-Certified-Solutions-Architect-Associate_Sample-Questions.pdf

AWS Ramp-Up Guide: Architect For AWS Cloud Architects, Solutions Architects, and Engineers [PDF File]. (n.d.). AWS Training. https://d1.awsstatic.com/training-and-certification/ramp-up-guides/RampUp_Architect_062020.pdf

AWS Whitepapers & Guides. (n.d.). AWS Training. https://aws.amazon.com/whitepapers/?whitepapers-main.sort-by=item.additionalFields.sortDate&whitepapers-main.sort-order=desc

Exam Readiness: AWS Certified Solutions Architect. (n.d.). AWS Training and Certification. https://aws.amazon.com/certification/certification-prep/

www.ingramcontent.com/pod-product-compliance
Lightning Source LLC
LaVergne TN
LVHW051742050326
832903LV00029B/2673